Growing Olives

Information on setting up your own olive growing enterprise

Dirk Dowling

This publication designed and edited by Mel Fielding
www.Melsart.com.au

Contents

For
Angele and Dick,
My Mum and Dad

Dirk Dowling is the owner of Trivengrove—an integrated olive farming business. It consists of a 200 acre farm and an Olive Shop in the township of Inglewood, Queensland. Trivengrove sells a wide range of Australian olive products, equipment for olive growers and also offers an extensive consultancy service.

Introduction

Trivengrove was established in 1999 after I made the decision to leave my public service career behind in Brisbane and move to the country. I don't think the decision was unusual in these times. However, my choice to grow olives was not considered mainstream farming and there were plenty of knockers at the time. When I made the move, I had 12 months research into olive growing under my belt and a great deal of enthusiasm to sustain me. However, I soon discovered farming is as much an art as any other involved profession and my time management skills needed refining for the country life. After many years now of consistently falling short of planned finish dates I have theorised that an estimate of time taken to complete a particular task should be multiplied by 2.5 to ensure completion on time. This is not news to experienced farmers, but for me it was learned behavior through trial and error.

The other thing I discovered was that being a farmer requires a range of skills not normally associated with basic farming. You need to understand the law, be an excellent administrator, know how to manage people, know something about agronomy, horticulture, first aid and above all you must be a problem solver. Don't misunderstand me though, I have never regretted my decision to pack in city living and throw all my time, energy and money into farming. I consider it the best decision I ever made. I have made some mistakes along the way and I have had to adjust my priorities more than once but I achieved what I set out to do - build a sustainable farming enterprise based around the existing new olive industry in Australia.

This introductory manual was written to provide prospective olive growers (both city people looking for a change in lifestyle and existing farmers) with information that may assist them to avoid some of the pitfalls and if nothing else understand what olive farming is about. It is not intended to be a detailed scientific study that contains all the answers.

Photo courtesy of the MacIntyre Gazette

Since I opened the Olive Shop to complement my farming enterprise, I have had many queries from people wanting to know more about growing the noble fruit. I hope this publication provides answers to some of the questions posed and points to some of the important areas that will require further research.

Dirk Dowling

C h a p t e r 1
The Olive Tree

The Olive Tree is a shallow rooted evergreen fruit tree that can live for thousands of years under the right conditions. It flowers in spring and begins bearing fruit in early summer.

The fruit is generally harvested in late Autumn to early Winter. There are hundreds of known varieties of olive tree in the world today. Although olive trees can be propagated from seeds, suckers, and even Ovuli, for the sake of consistency and practicality, most commercial olive trees are propagated from hardwood cuttings (some varieties must be grafted).

The tree has a tendency to grow as a bush and can regenerate where damage occurs through frost or otherwise. It readily sends out shoots from the base and trunk of the tree (suckers) and this can be problematic under commercial growing conditions (see later). Trees grow rapidly under the right conditions and can record growth rates in excess of one metre per year. Most olive varieties bear fruit 3-4 years after planting approximately 18 month old trees. Some varieties are susceptible to alternate bearing habits. The bark on the olive tree is quite thin and can be damaged easily if care is not taken. Several commentators have suggested that most varieties are self-pollinating, but some growers have experienced increased yields where pollinators have been interplanted with the main variety. Pollination research is currently being undertaken at several institutions around Australia. Some recent results have suggested that the Frantoio variety may be one of the best overall pollinators.

Photo courtesy of the MacIntyre Gazette

The olive tree is extremely hardy, but it does require irrigation to produce commercial yields in Australia. Growers should be careful not to overwater their trees (See Chapter 8). With the right care and attention the tree can grow rapidly and produce high yields.

The olive tree can live for thousands of years. There are several ancient trees living currently in the Garden of Gethsemane, believed to be over 2000 years old. These trees were probably alive at the time of Christ, and they still bear fruit.

Chapter 2
Industry Overview

The olive tree has been farmed for centuries, mainly in Mediterranean countries such as Spain and Italy. However, olives are rapidly being recognised as a profitable crop in other parts of the world such as Argentina, South Africa and even Australia.

Olive trees have been in Australia since settlement. However, it has only been in the past decade that olive farming has moved away from being a boutique industry and moved towards becoming a major industry in Australia.

There are currently over 50 regional olive associations in Australia with over 600 members. Olives are being grown in Queensland, New South Wales, Victoria, South Australia, Western Australia and even Tasmania.

In the past decade, several large corporate interests (such as the Barkworth Group with its Viva brand of olives) have provided the catalyst for new growers to enter the industry and for existing growers to increase plantings. These corporate interests offer investment packages to clients as tax effective investment opportunities. Under the schemes, individuals purchase a set number of trees in large corporate groves. They pay for grove maintenance, trademark rights, processing rights etc. Excess profits are returned to them.

These investment packages have resulted in large injections of capital into the industry and the flow on benefits have seen more processing facilities available, increased marketing in Australia and overseas, and subsequently a ready market for olive growers to sell their fruit. The result has been a move away from the boutique industry of the past into a more mainstream industry with enormous potential to grow rapidly and become sustainable in the long term. The health benefits of olives are being widely promoted at the moment and this has aided in the recent transformation of the industry. Olive consumption in Australia is currently worth approximately 120 million dollars per year. Of this amount Australia imports over 95% from overseas. Many opportunities exist for import replacement and export opportunities are successfully being pursued.

HANDY HINT Processors are becoming more fussy about the farm operations that supply them fruit. Quality control is being recognised as a vital requirement for these operations to ensure that the fruit purchased is of the highest standard. The Department of Primary Industries in Queensland has created the *Olive Care* program to teach growers about these issues and provide them with appropriate certification. I recommend that this course be undertaken by all prospective olive growers. It will become increasingly difficult to sell your fruit without certification and, apart from anything else, the course provides a range of valuable information that will assist you to operate a sustainable and profitable operation.

The olive tree is the international symbol of peace, joy and happiness. As part of the NASA program a gold-plated olive branch was placed on the moon.

There are many business issues new olive farmers must confront prior to planting their grove. Some of the more obvious ones are as follows:

Business Plan

A Business Plan is vital. It should be based on your own research into olive growing. This document will assist you to plan your venture properly and can also be provided to the Tax Office (see below).

Zoning Laws

Land needs to be designated to allow for agricultural uses. If you are thinking about a processing plant in the future, make sure the zoning also allow this enterprise.

Irrigation

Make sure the property has enough dam water or prospective dam sites to accommodate your requirements. If not, research the requirements for drilling a bore and/or drawing from a water course. Contact your local Department of Natural Resources (DNR) office to arrange an inspection of the property to discuss the legal requirements for dams, bore drilling and river/creek allocations. Apply for a water licence immediately, even if you are not intending to drill or draw water straight away (Your licence can be extended for a 2 year period or more).

Tax

If you are not an existing farmer, ask your accountant to arrange for a Private Ruling with the Tax Office and provide him/her with your Business Plan (Under the current legislation if you earn over $40,000 of income from activities off-farm, you must satisfy one of several criteria to be able to claim your expenses from the olive venture. One of these criteria allows for the Tax Commissioner to waive the requirement if it can be shown that the enterprise will be profitable/sustainable after a certain period of time).

Rates

Check with your local Council to see if your property is classified as a house block. If it is you will be paying higher rates than a farming property. Talk to your DNR representative about a revaluation of the property based on your olive growing activities. In Queensland, there are several criteria under the legislation that allow for the reduced rateable value. One is the expenditure of over $50,000 on farm improvements and various works.

There are many more issues involved in setting up your olive venture. I have tried to point out here some of the more obvious ones.

HANDY HINT By employing experts in the various fields you can save a great deal of time and money and avoid more serious mistakes.

An olive tree can grow over one metre every year under the right conditions. The trees normally bear fruit in the fourth year after planting. However, some of the growers in this region have seen fruit well before that.

Chapter 4

Choosing Your Grove Site

Olive trees will grow in a variety of soil types as long as good drainage is present and the pH level of the soil is between 6.5 and 8. The topography of your site may assist with the drainage. However, be careful not to assume that sloping ground has good drainage and remember that the steeper the ground the harder it will be to harvest effectively.

Your site should have some wind protection. However, do not plant your olive trees too close to surrounding bushland (minimum 15 metres distance). Competition for water can cause olive trees to suffer if they are planted too close to other trees. Make sure there is easy access to the site for machinery and other equipment.

Most olive tree varieties can be planted at 8m x 5m spacing (i.e., rows are 8 metres apart and trees are 5 metres apart). This will ensure that each tree has access to sufficient water to assist with optimum growth. The spacing also allows easy access for harvesting.

You can plant the trees closer if you intend to prune monoconically. This method requires trellising work to support the trees. There are other configurations for planting olive trees. These should be researched to provide you with the optimum layout for your purposes.

The site must allow for rows to be planted approximately North—South as this will allow for the best penetration of sunlight. Consideration must also be given to distance from the water source as the further away the grove is from the source, the greater the expense to transport the water to the trees.

HANDY HINT Having a full soil test done and discussing your options with an agronomist can save you a lot of time, effort and money in the long run.

Olives ripen from green to black during the fruiting cycle. However, not all varieties are acceptable as black ripe fruit and must be harvested once they are green ripe.

Chapter 5
Choosing Your Varieties

Variety selection is important to the success of your enterprise. Several factors are relevant here. Your choices will depend in large part on whether you intend to sell or process your olives for oil or table fruit. It is important to understand that certain varieties will give you higher oil content than others in your particular growing conditions, while still other varieties are more suitable for pickling. There are other factors to consider. The flavour of certain olive varieties can be in demand despite the fact that the variety itself only produces minimal oil content. Many blends of oils are just that - a blend of several varieties to come up with the final product.

Research is continuing in many parts of Australia to discover what the optimum varieties are for different olive growing areas. Some commentators have suggested that the choices growers make in this area will become the key to the success or otherwise of the industry here in Australia.

It is impossible to give details here on all the varieties available to growers and the potential benefits of choosing particular ones, as each growers situation will be different. However, I can mention some of the successes and apparent failures in the Inglewood Region to date:

Most growers are finding that under our conditions the Manzanillo variety is not producing the expected 20% + oil content when processed. However, as a table variety the Manzanillo grows well in this region and the trees are cropping quite heavily.

Most growers are very happy with the Frantoio and Corregiolla varieties. The oil is of a high quality and the oil content is also high. The trees crop quite heavily.

Most growers are finding that the variety Hardy's Mammoth is taking a long time to bear fruit (some growers have 5 year old trees that have not produced fruit yet) and some growers are finding that the true Kalamata variety is taking a long time to get going.

Virgin Olive Oil:

Manufactured from whole, ripe, undamaged olives without heat. An unrefined oil that still contains many factors unique to olives.

Chapter 6
Land Preparation

There are several necessary steps to land preparation for growing olive trees. The trees grow best in a pH of 6.5 to 8. Therefore if your level is outside this range you will need to add either gypsum or lime to achieve the required pH. It is important to note that adjusting the pH this way may only be a temporary solution. By adding mulch and building up the organic carbon in your soil after planting you will inevitably begin to change the pH again to a more acidic level.

Although the olive tree is shallow rooted, it is a good idea to maintain a reasonable soil profile for optimum root growth. If your available root depth is impeded by a hard layer or clay pan, you should have the soil ripped prior to planting. This will break up the layer and allow for better root penetration and drainage. Mounding is also an option here, particularly if you have poor draining soil.

You will also need to add well rotted manure. Many growers are also adding crusher dust prior to planting their trees. Detailed research into the benefits of crusher dust are not available yet. However, many believe the rock dust releases minerals over a long period of time which aid in the growth of the trees. If you do use the dust, make sure it is just that 'dust'. The finer the material the better. It is a good idea to have all these materials spread on the surface prior to ripping. Doing it this way will ensure that the manure etc finds its way deeper into the soil and does not accumulate merely in the top soil.

Ensure that your grove surface is relatively level before putting your trees in. This will ensure you have no problems slashing the grass in between the rows. Irrigation works must be done prior to planting (See Chapter 7). If you leave it until after the trees are in it is more difficult to maneuver around the

grove and you can even damage some of your trees in the process. I made the decision to have my fencing completely finished before I began preparing the soil. I recommend this approach. Water run-off and erosion will be detrimental to your trees therefore it is a good idea to establish some sort of cover in between your rows at the earliest opportunity. Some growers are trying cover crops between their rows, where they have enough available water. Others (like me) are happy for the native grasses to do the job.

Extra Virgin Olive Oil:

"Extra Virgin" means that this form of olive oil only contains the highest quality olives and that strict guidelines have been followed in the oil's manufacture

Olive trees are not irrigated in most Mediterranean situations. The olive tree will survive without irrigation under these dryland conditions, however lower yields and slower growth rates do result from this method. The success of the industry in Australia and our ability to compete with overseas is based on the implementation of the new irrigated method. The correct irrigation of the orchard is therefore one of the most important aspects of olive growing in this country.

Olive trees need a large amount of water to produce heavy crops. However, in the early years the requirement is less than at full maturity. You should ensure that your estimates on water requirements are based on mature trees to ensure sufficient availability in later years. It is impossible to estimate the requirements for all situations. Some commentators have suggested that a mature olive tree requires between 6 - 10 megalitres of water per hectare per year (250 trees at 5m x 8m spacing). This includes rainfall and will vary depending on your particular topography, soil type, weather, evaporation rates, ground cover, age of the tree etc.

We have irrigated our younger trees by applying between 50 to 75 litres per week per tree. We irrigate in short bursts to allow for good infiltration and to avoid too much water escaping below the root zone. Some growers in the area with more mature trees and different soil types are supplying at least 75 to 100+ litres per week per tree. These figures are based on mid-summer conditions. Winter watering will be a good deal less than these rates.

It is important to ensure that each tree has its own individual sprinkler as this will ensure consistent application rates (adjustable sprinklers can supply various amounts per hour) and more accurate placement. Be aware that depending on wind and other weather conditions evaporation rates may be very high if you are using sprinklers. Seek advice from a specialist on these matters. You can either bury your mains and laterals (polypipe) or lay them on the surface. There are benefits and detriments to doing it either way.

HANDY HINTS It is a good idea to have some sort of flushing system on your irrigation setup. This will allow you to flush the system regularly to avoid silt and algae build up in your lines. Also, consider using a soil moisture monitoring system (such as Tensiometers). The majority of growers in this area do. The right system can save you thousands of litres of water and a lot of guesswork. Government rebates are currently available for primary producers for irrigation equipment in all Australian States.

Non-Virgin or Refined Olive Oil:

Refined, deodorized, degummed and bleached using heat. This form of olive oil has been subjected to nutrient loss and molecular changes that are detrimental to human health.

Chapter 8
Planting and Staking

Planting your olive trees is not a difficult process. The only difficulty usually relates to the numbers involved and therefore the time it takes. We found that with the right preparation we could comfortably plant and secure approximately 75 trees every 1.5 hours. We did this with three people.

We started by placing a tree and stake at each site. We then had one person pound in the stakes followed by the next person planting the tree and the last person securing the trees to the stakes. We did not tease out the roots of the trees when they were removed from the pots as we believe this damages the fine root hairs. You should note that some commentators have suggested that the trees will do better if planted well below the surface level, while other commentators have recommended against this approach.

We planted our trees at a depth slightly below the ground level and we left a slight depression around the tree to trap more water. To ensure good root penetration of the soil it is a good idea to make sure that when you dig the hole to plant you are careful not to leave a smooth surface around the edges of the hole. When the tree is in the ground be sure to press down lightly around the roots to remove air pockets and minimise the risk of the roots being exposed. We watered each site prior to planting. This assisted with digging the hole. Immediately after planting we gave each site a good water also. It is a good idea to mulch each tree site as this will help to conserve water, prevent erosion, reduce weeds and add organic carbon to the soil as the mulch breaks down.

We used spoilt lucerne as it breaks down quite quickly and adds nitrogen to assist with growth. We avoided dibbling or adding any starter fertilisers at planting as we believed the manure, crusher dust and lime was a sufficient package.

We did however add some NPK as our soil test indicated this would be a good idea. We initially used bamboo stakes to support the trees and a tape gun to secure them to the stake. Olive trees require a strong root system to thrive and the stakes allowed the tree to sway in the wind. The belief here is that with too rigid a support the tree will not sense the need to develop a strong root system. The bamboo stakes did not last long and we ended up replacing them with hardwood stakes. By using flexible tree ties in a figure eight configuration we were able keep the trees away from the stakes and allow for each one to flex in the wind anyway.

HANDY HINT Avoid planting too close to your water source if there is a chance of flooding the grove. Olive trees are extremely hardy. However, wet feet can kill them quite rapidly.

Virgin Olive Oil and Extra Virgin Olive Oil are the only mass market commercial oils that have not been heated to temperatures above 150°C during their manufacture.

Chapter 9
Grove Maintenance

Many growers believe that in the early years the control of weeds takes up most of their time in the grove. Mulching heavily can assist to keep weeds under control and some growers have even tried weed matting. I have found that good mulching practice and regular doses of *glyphosate* (Roundup) does a lot to alleviate the problem. Another concern is sucker growth. As mentioned previously, the olive tree likes to send out shoots from its root system and from its trunk. Suckers should be taken off immediately.

The aim with the tree is to have a clear trunk to about 1 metre.

Recommendations for the industry were to maintain the clear trunk to allow for the attachment of tree shaker equipment. Technology has moved ahead quite rapidly over the past decade and this option may now be superseded by overhead harvesters that cause less damage to the tree. The clear trunk is still a good idea though. It assists with preventing pests gaining easy access to the tree via branches hanging on the ground. It also allows for easier weeding at the base and easier access to hand harvesting equipment (such as olive catchers on wheels).

Pruning should be kept to a minimum in the early years. The more leaf material taken off the tree the less photosynthesis can take place and hence the slower the growth rate will be. However, growers should be careful not to leave undesirable lateral branching where this growth can take away nutrients from the main leader. Pruning is quite an art. The various methods and practices can be taught to a certain extent.

Photo courtesy of the MacIntyre Gazette

Most growers will learn by doing and will use the basic principles as a guide only to their situation. You will find in the early years in particular that maintenance of the trees and the irrigation system is an ongoing exercise. Each time you go into the grove you will find blocked sprinklers, sucker growth, trees that need retying etc. It is a good idea to bring all the necessary equipment with you each time you enter your grove. Spare ties, sprinkler heads, secateurs etc.

Olive oil is a poor source of Essential Fatty Acids which should be supplied from other dietary oils, but most of its other constituents are beneficial and have not been "deformed" by industrial processing.

Chapter 10
Pest and Disease Problems

There are some pest & disease problems with olive trees, such as Olive Lace Bug, Scale and Mite. Some farmers have had problems with birds (mainly parrots) chewing off new shoots and some even picking at the fruit. Some farmers have also had problems with kangaroos, particularly in drought affected areas. I have seen kangaroos chewing leaves from low hanging branches and even chewing the bark on newly planted trees. Some disease problems can also affect growth/production. Verticilium Wilt can cause whole sections of the tree to die off and detrimental fungi such as *Cycloconium oleaginum* (Peacock Spot) causes leaf damage which can lead to reduced yields if not taken care of.

To combat some of these problems the Government has authorised the use of certain chemicals for olive growers (Information can be obtained by contacting the Department of Primary Industries in your State).

It is important to note that in Australia, unlike overseas, many of the more dangerous diseases are not found. For instance the disease Olive Knot caused by *Pseudomonas syringae* has not been found in Australia to date.

Pest and disease problems for olive growing in Australia are not generally problematic. Spot spraying in smaller orchards is generally sufficient to control cyclic events. Animal problems can be overcome with suitable fencing. Bird problems are a little more difficult to manage. However, most growers would agree that the damage caused by them is minimal anyway.

I have personally found that the best treatment for disease problems is to maintain healthy trees. If the tree is strong and healthy it can resist most infestations and/or minimise their effects.

Olive oil is pressed from the flesh of the olive (Olea europaea), derived from the olive fruit rather than its seed.

Chapter 11
Establishment and Maintenance Costs

Individual conditions will dictate the actual expenses involved in setting up your enterprise. You may already own the land or you may have to purchase it. You may have good access roads or you may be dealing with virgin bush or complete regrowth. For the purposes of this introductory edition I can only provide indicative costs. I will concentrate only on those costs for the actual grove setup itself. Other expenses will need further research and will in each case be site specific. Where I have quoted actual prices I have given the higher of the estimated quotes in all cases.

The costs for setting up and maintaining an olive grove are spread across the following areas:

- Site Development
- Land Preparation
- Irrigation
- Planting
- Maintenance

SITE DEVELOPMENT

Heavy machinery may be needed to clear bushland, create roads, level blocks, create contours, create mounding, build dams etc. I have found that Graders/Bulldozers etc can be hired for between $90.00 to $120.00 per hour (depending on the distance of travel to reach your property, size of machinery, size of the job etc).

Fencing costs will vary depending on the materials and configurations used. I used 2m hardwood posts at eight metre intervals covered by hinge joint fencing wire standing at 90cm, with two strands of barbed wire above the hinge joint. My cost per metre worked out to approximately $2.00.

Photo courtesy of the MacIntyre Gazette

LAND PREPARATION

I had a basic soil test done by an agronomist. This cost me $150.00 which included an analysis of the results. I recommend a more complex analysis for anyone contemplating planting over 500 trees. A detailed examination can show up differences across a variety of soil conditions and can highlight areas that require special attention before planting. Costs for this service can vary considerably.

You can mark out the grove yourself or you can employ a surveyor to do the job. If you have any drainage works that are needed and/

or the irrigation is complex enough to require the services of a surveyor then you should have the job done properly. Rates vary widely for these services and are totally dependant on your particular requirements. I will assume for these costings that you do not require this service.

You may also need to treat weeds prior to planting your trees. This will involve spraying out the weeds (and maybe even the grasses). Costs for this exercise will vary depending on what equipment you have available and whether you actually hire someone to do the job. I will assume for these costings that you have the equipment needed to spray the rows before planting, you do the job yourself and you are leaving the grasses in between the rows of trees (cost is therefore negligible).

Soil preparation is vital to the success of your enterprise. Depending on the results of your soil test, its type and condition most growers will, at the very least, need to add well rotted manure, lime or gypsum (to raise or lower the pH) and crusher dust to the soil prior to planting.

Well rotted manure will generally cost $10.00 -$15.00 per cubic metre delivered. Each cubic metre will cover approximately 12 trees. This means that with 250 trees per hectare it will cost up to $312.00 per hectare. The manure will need to be spread. If you hire someone to do this it will add further cost to the exercise. I will assume for these costings that you have the equipment needed to do the job yourself.

Lime will cost you between $20.00-$30.00 per tonne depending on the distance to deliver, quantity ordered etc. You will need approximately 1.6 tonnes per hectare ($48.00). As with the manure, you will need to spread the lime and this may add further costs. I will assume for these costings that you have the

equipment needed to do the job yourself. (Note that no costings for gypsum application were available at the time of writing).

Crusher dust will cost you between $15.00-$25.00 per tonne delivered, depending on distance to deliver, quantity ordered etc. 1 cubic metre is sufficient for 12 tree sites. You will need to spread approximately 31 tonnes per hectare. At $25.00 this amounts to approximately $775.00 per hectare. As with the manure and lime I will assume you have the equipment needed to do the job of spreading it yourself.

It is a good idea to have these additives ripped in to your rows prior to planting. This will ensure that the material is spread through the soil profile and is not limited to the top soil area.

Deep ripping by a bulldozer with sufficiently deep tines (600mm or longer) is recommended. The rows should be ripped in a strip at least 3 m wide. The cost for this exercise (per hectare) at approximately $90.00 -$120.00 per hour will be $240.00.

You may also need to level out your rows once the ripping is complete and depending on your drainage requirements you may also need to create mounding. These costs will be additional. I will assume for these costings that you have the equipment to level out your rows after ripping and that no mounding is required.

IRRIGATION

I am unable to give accurate estimates on irrigation costs as these will vary greatly depending on your water source and the number of trees you plant. There are other variables depending on your situation, such as the number of joiners required for your configuration of polypiping, the size of your pump, the type of sprinklers you use, whether you bury your piping or lay it on the surface etc. I can say that my irrigation costs for setting up my first grove of 250 trees which draws water from a dam less than 500 metres from the grove was approximately $2000.00. I used a 6 hp pump. My polypiping consists of 2 inch mains and 1 inch laterals. I planted at 8m x 5m spacing. I had 10 rows with 25 trees in each row and I used individual sprinklers ($2.50 each) for each tree. Costs will increase considerably if you have someone install the irrigation for you. For these costings I will assume you do the work yourself and you use a similar configuration to mine. Your total cost should come in at around $2000.00 for the first hectare (250 trees) and assuming your pump can also handle the next 250 trees, the cost for the second grove will be approximately $1500.00. I also recommend using a soil moisture monitoring system. Tensiometers are reasonably priced and very efficient. Costs vary depending on your requirements. With Government rebates currently available a good set for your first 250 trees can cost as little as $400.00.

PLANTING

The olive trees themselves will cost approximately $5.00-$6.00 each (including delivery charges). These costs are for trees at 60cm-90cm height that are sun hardened and ready for planting. Certain grafted varieties will cost more. Therefore 250 trees will cost you $1500.00.

The labour costs for planting your trees may be quite high depending on the number of trees you intend to plant. For these costings I will assume you are planting the trees yourself (no labour cost).

As stated previously I recommend using hardwood stakes. 250 stakes will cost you approximately $240.00. It is a good idea to invest in a tape tool to secure your young trees at planting (you can use stronger material later on to secure them once they start growing). A tapetool set will cost between $90.00-$120.00.

Mulching your newly planted trees is vital to their optimum growth. I used spoilt lucerne. 1 bale covered approximately 5 trees. Costs per bale will vary depending on availability. I picked up my first 50 bales at $1.50 each. However, I have paid up to $2.50 a bale since. Total cost for 250 trees is therefore $125.00.

MAINTENANCE

These costs will vary depending on your particular circumstances. However, certain equipment needs to be purchased initially and there are some ongoing costs that will be constant. It is a good idea to purchase a good set of secateurs and tree loppers (approximately $170.00). I also recommend you purchase a note book of some kind to keep notes each time you enter the grove. It is difficult to get around the grove (depending on its size) without a motorbike or appropriate transport (small Ag-bike $4000.00 new) and if you don't have the right equipment, you will need to purchase a backpack spray unit for applying roundup to your weeds ($264.00 new). Depending on the size of your operation it may be more cost effective to purchase a Quad bike complete with spray unit (approximately $12,000 new). This will certainly save you time and back ache. You will also need to purchase pest & disease monitoring equipment such as magnifying lenses, pest traps and photo literature for identification (approximately $100.00).

Depending on the size of your operation and your circumstances I recommend you either have access to or buy a small tractor with a 3 pint linkage setup. There are many attachments that the tractor can operate such as a slasher, post hole digger and even a ripper. Costs will vary depending on whether you purchase the tractor new or used. I bought a second hand tractor for $10,000 (28 horsepower) and I consider it has been the best investment I made for my enterprise to date.

Mulch will need to be added regularly and you will need to add fertilisers to your trees. You can either add them directly to the soil or consider using a fertigation method. For the latter you will need to purchase an appropriate setup for your irrigation system. In some situations manure will be added each year also.

You will need to have a leaf analysis done at least once every year. Costs vary with different organisations for this service.

However, you can count on spending approximately $75.00-$150.00, depending on your requirements.

There are many other incidental costs you will come across as your enterprise takes shape. I am unable to canvass all of them in this brief publication. I have attempted to give you some idea of the types of costs involved. Your particular circumstances will dictate how close my quotes are to your own costs and your location may affect the costings a great deal.

Specialty Olive Shop Opens in Inglewood *Trivengrove*

❑ Mel Fielding and Dirk Dowling from Trivengrove Inglewood with a sample of olive products in store. The new business opens this Saturday and will stock a wide range of olive related products. The shop will cater for the olive grower, local residents and the passing tourist trade. Also available at Trivengrove will be business/consultancy, desk top publishing and web page design services.

MacIntyre Gazette 25 October 2001

Assuming these circumstances are true:

- there is easy access to your grove and no roads need to be created;
- your grove site has been cleared;
- there are no requirements for mounding, contour creation or a special irrigation setup;
- your water supply is close to your grove site and only requires the purchase of a small firefighters pump;
- you are going to plant 250 trees at 8m x 5m spacing;
- you will be doing all the labour yourself;
- you have a tractor, slasher, post hole digger, spreader and a range of other equipment;

then the following estimates will be relevant to your startup costs for 250 olive trees:

Site Development
[Fencing = $800.00]

Land Preparation
[Soil Test = $150.00, Manure = $312.00, Lime = $48.00, Crusher Dust = $775.00, Deep Ripping = $240.00]

Irrigation
[First 250 = $2000.00]

Planting
[Trees = $1500.00, Stakes = $240.00, Tapetool set = $120.00, Mulch = $125.00]

Maintenance
[Secateurs and Tree Loppers = $170.00, Backpack Spray Unit = $264.00, Pest & Disease Monitoring Equipment = $120.00

The total cost of setting up an olive grove of 250 olive trees in these circumstances will be approximately $6,864.00

Please note that these costs are applicable in 2002

Olive oil:

- Contains substances that possess Antioxidant properties
- Inhibits abnormal blood clotting by lowering plasma fibrinogen levels
- Neutralizes dietary cholesterol, preventing it from entering the bloodstream
- Decreases serum LDL cholesterol
- Increases serum HDL cholesterol
- Reduces the production of cholesterol gallstones due to oleoeuropein
- Lowers blood pressure in persons afflicted with hypertension – in scientific research, 1 tablespoon per day reduced blood pressure by 5 systolic point and 4 diastolic points
- Assists the development of cell membranes, cell formation and cell differentiation
- Stimulates the secretion of bile
- Alleviates constipation (although excessive consumption can cause temporary mild diarrhoea)
- Lowers the risk of developing breast cancer – incidence of breast cancer is lower in females who consume olive oil more than once per day
- Applied topically: alleviates bruising, accelerates the healing of calluses, helps to soften dandruff thereby facilitating its elimination, alleviates mastalgia (painful breasts)
- Alleviates eczema (where the eczema is due to deficiency of fatty acids)

Chapter 12

Conclusion

I have attempted to explain what olive growing in Australia is like at the moment and what it involves. I have tried to point out some of the more important areas new growers need to research as part of their planning process. I understand that it is difficult to get an initial impression of a new industry and whether it is right for you without some idea of the costs involved. I have therefore set out some estimates on what a new grower might expect under a particular scenario. These figures are not accurate enough to form the basis of any business decision. Particularly since the variables are too numerous to mention. They are merely provided to give the reader some general idea of whether olive growing is right for them under their current circumstances and hopefully will promote further more accurate research on the basis that the costs do seem reasonable.

I believe the olive industry in Australia is in a strong position at the moment and that it will continue to expand on its current solid foundations in the future. More growers are needed to supply the current and future demands of processors. Our ability to compete with overseas products and therefore capture a larger slice of the $120 million worth of imports will depend as much on the availability of produce as the conditions concerning tariffs and subsidies being paid to overseas growers. The Australian olive industry is going through a strong growth phase at the moment that is set to last for many years.

I encourage existing farmers looking to diversify and others looking for a sustainable and profitable enterprise to consider planting olives. It is not a get rich quick enterprise. However, Australia now has a strong industry presence and farming olives can offer a profitable and enjoyable lifestyle.

CPSIA information can be obtained at www.ICGtesting.com
Printed in the USA
BVIW12n1419041116
466948BV00018B/260